The *Physical* Brain

By
Faith Brynie

Scientific Consultant:
Dr. Paul Thompson
Assistant Professor of Neurology, UCLA

BLACKBIRCH PRESS, INC.
WOODBRIDGE, CONNECTICUT

Published by Blackbirch Press, Inc.
260 Amity Road
Woodbridge, CT 06525
Web site: http://www.blackbirch.com
e-mail: staff@blackbirch.com
© 2001 Blackbirch Press, Inc.

Printed in Belgium

10 9 8 7 6 5 4 3 2 1

Photo credits:
Cover (background), pages 4, 6, 16, 20, 28 (boy), 29 (boy), 33–34, 38–39,
41–42, 45, 48, 51, 53–54, 58–59: PhotoDisc; cover (inset), back cover, 7–8,
12, 25, 28 (brain), 29 (brain), 37, 49, 52: LifeArt; pages 10–11, 14, 24, 57:
Corel Corporation; pages 13, 23, 26, 31, 46, 50, 56: Blackbirch Press, Inc.;
page 30: PhotoSpin.

Library of Congress Cataloging-in-Publication Data
Brynie, Faith Hickman, 1946–
Physical brain / by Faith Brynie.
        p. cm. — (The amazing brain)
Includes index.
        ISBN 1-56711-424-5 (hardcover)
1. Brain—Juvenile literature. 2. Neurophysiology—Juvenile literature.
3. Neuroanatomy—Juvenile literature. [1. Brain.] I. Title. II. Amazing
brain series.

QP361.5 .B79 2001   00-011947
612. 8'2—dc21

Table of Contents

Chapter 1

Brain Watching

Are you a brain watcher? Look closely as a dog bounds after a Frisbee, a hummingbird sips nectar from a blossom, or a goldfish circles a pond. In each case, you are seeing behavior. You are also seeing a brain in action!

The leaping, drinking, and swimming occur because nerve cells "fire," triggering coordinated movements of legs, wings, or fins. The control center for the action is the brain. There, many signals arrive from the senses. Messages carried by nerves to the brain tell the dog its position in space, the bird the location of a fragrant blossom, and the fish its depth in the water. Messages also travel out from the brain. They direct and coordinate action. Nerve impulses let the dog leap on target. They spark the bird's flight to the sweetest flowers and the fish's hasty retreat to the depths whenever danger threatens.

Brains and Behaviors

No brain is simple. Behaviors are never simple either. Worms, insects, and soft-bodied ocean creatures respond to their environments in sophisticated ways. Clusters of nerve cells that serve as brains let these animals find food, escape predators, survive, and reproduce.

But the more complex the brain, the greater the range of behaviors. For example, reptiles such as lizards and snakes have brains much like the brain stem of human beings. Their brains monitor and control basic life processes, such as breathing and heartbeat. The reptilian brain controls food-seeking, eating, mating, and reproduction. It also oversees communication and social interactions among individuals and groups.

Still more complex are mammals that can maintain a constant body temperature. They have another brain area much like the human limbic system. That system controls the blood's pressure and sugar content. It also spurs action in the face of danger,

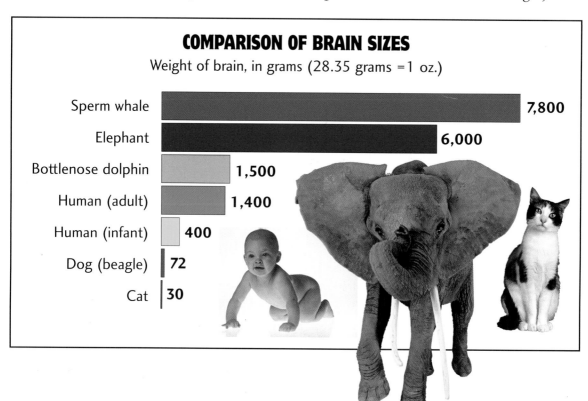

COMPARISON OF BRAIN SIZES

Weight of brain, in grams (28.35 grams =1 oz.)

Sperm whale	7,800
Elephant	6,000
Bottlenose dolphin	1,500
Human (adult)	1,400
Human (infant)	400
Dog (beagle)	72
Cat	30

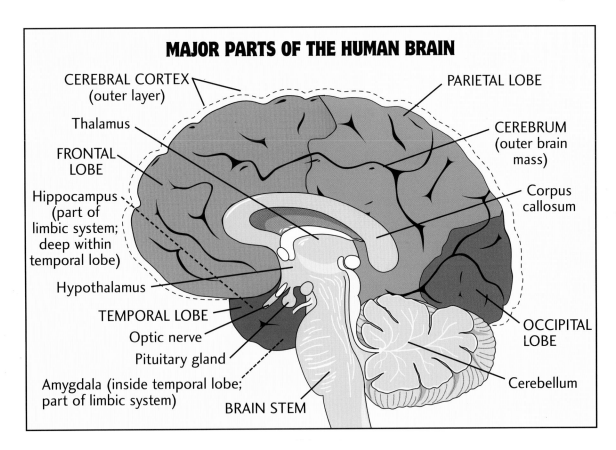

MAJOR PARTS OF THE HUMAN BRAIN

CEREBRAL CORTEX
(outer layer)

PARIETAL LOBE

Thalamus

CEREBRUM
(outer brain
mass)

FRONTAL
LOBE

Corpus
callosum

Hippocampus
(part of
limbic system;
deep within
temporal lobe)

Hypothalamus

TEMPORAL LOBE

OCCIPITAL
LOBE

Optic nerve

Pituitary gland

Cerebellum

Amygdala (inside temporal lobe;
part of limbic system)

BRAIN STEM

often called the "fight or flight" response. When a mother bear defends her cubs (fight) or a deer runs from a bobcat (flight), the limbic system is in charge.

Humans and other primates have yet another brain area, the cerebrum. This two-lobed structure looks a little like a cauliflower. It processes information from the senses. It also directs a variety of behaviors that are more advanced than those of reptiles, birds, or other mammals. For example, primates use tools, learn complex behaviors, and rear their young for long periods. Some cooperate in social groups.

In human beings, the thin outer layer of the cerebrum is called the cortex. The cortex is the center of thought, expression, decision-making, and purpose. Humans share much of their brain structure with other animals, but the cortex directs the behaviors that make human beings unique, such as building tools, using language, and planning for the future.

Blueprint of a Brain

The brain stem controls basic body functions. It keeps air moving in and out of the lungs. It sends signals that keep the brain awake. It keeps the heart beating and food digesting. It controls the removal of poisonous wastes from the blood and holds body temperature constant—except when infection threatens. Then it turns on the fever response. The brain stem handles all these functions silently. No conscious thought or action is needed.

No conscious control is needed for many movements either. Once motor skills are learned, they can be performed without conscious effort. That's because the cerebellum, a small section

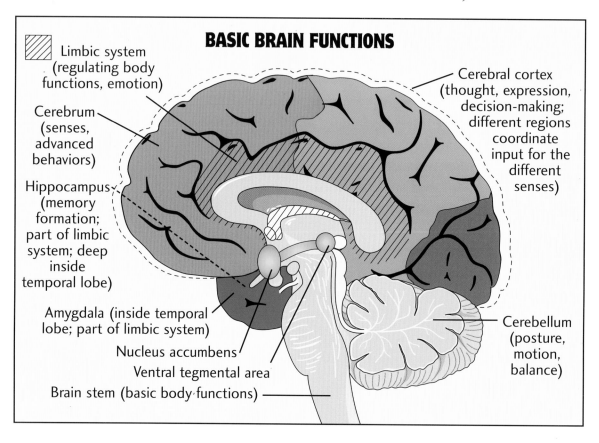

BASIC BRAIN FUNCTIONS

Limbic system (regulating body functions, emotion)

Cerebrum (senses, advanced behaviors)

Hippocampus (memory formation; part of limbic system; deep inside temporal lobe)

Amygdala (inside temporal lobe; part of limbic system)

Nucleus accumbens

Ventral tegmental area

Brain stem (basic body functions)

Cerebral cortex (thought, expression, decision-making; different regions coordinate input for the different senses)

Cerebellum (posture, motion, balance)

at the "bottom" of the brain, takes over. It handles posture, motion, and balance in every situation, from riding a roller coaster to standing on your head. It also takes over learned movements, large and small. That explains why riding a bicycle may seem difficult at first but becomes automatic with practice.

The limbic system lies above the cerebellum. It is not a single structure, but several. The organs of the limbic system work with the brain stem in regulating temperature, blood pressure, heart rate, and blood sugar. Two parts of the limbic system, the hippocampus and the amygdala, are essential to forming memories. In humans, the limbic system is also the center of emotions. If you cry over an old movie or laugh at silly jokes, your limbic system is at work.

The limbic system is part of the cerebrum. The two hemispheres of the cerebrum control movements on opposite sides of the body. For example, information from the right eye goes to the left side of the brain. And the brain's right side directs movement of the left hand. But the two halves do not work independently. A bundle of nerve fibers connects the hemispheres. This bundle, the corpus callosum, shuttles messages back and forth between the sides.

The cerebrum's thin outer layer, the cortex, processes input from the senses. Different areas of the cortex manage sight, hearing, taste, smell, and touch. Along with parts of the limbic system, the cortex makes and stores memories. It directs voluntary movement, speaking, reading, and conscious thought.

DIAGRAM OF A NEURON

dendrites

cell body

axon

MOTOR NEURON

NEURON IN THE CEREBRAL CORTEX

Brain Cells

Like all other parts of the human body, the brain is made of cells. About ten percent are nerve cells, called neurons. Neurons send, carry, and receive messages, or nerve impulses. The cell body of a neuron is roughly spherical, but thin fibers stretch out from it. One long fiber, the axon, carries messages away from the cell body. Smaller, shorter and more numerous fibers, called dendrites, carry messages toward the cell body.

Motor neurons carry messages from the brain or spinal cord to the muscles, causing them to contract. Some motor neurons control actions that are automatic and unconscious, such as the blinking of eyelids or the muscular contractions that propel food through the digestive system. Other motor neurons trigger voluntary action, such as picking up a pencil or kicking a ball.

Sensory neurons carry messages from the sense organs to the brain and spinal cord. For example, cells in the retina of the eye, called cones, respond to wavelengths of visible light. When stimulated, they send messages that the brain interprets as the colors of the spectrum. Roses are red and violets are blue only because the brain processes wavelengths in that way. Other

Cells in the retina—called cones—respond to wavelengths of visible light, which the brain interprets as "color."

visual cells send signals that the brain deciphers as movement, line, edge, or distance.

The other 90 percent of brain cells are called glial cells or glia. Glia support neurons and play a role in brain repair. They regulate the speed of nerve impulses. Some scientists think they are essential to the correct wiring of the brain. Without glia, neurons are inefficient communicators and often fail to pass messages along. With the support of glial cells, however, neuronal action rarely fails, and signals are strong.

Thousands of tiny blood vessels supply the brain with food and oxygen and carry away wastes. Inside these vessels lies a network of tightly packed cells called the blood-brain barrier. This barrier prevents harmful chemicals and disease-causing organisms from entering brain cells. It acts as the brain's "gatekeeper," blocking molecules that do not dissolve in fat. It also actively ferries essential molecules, such as glucose (sugar) and vitamin C, into brain cells.

Running a Body

No matter what the animal, a brain's first job is running a body. Bundles of neurons called nerve fibers manage the back-and-forth communication necessary to do that job.

Your body and brain are in constant communication to keep your body running properly.

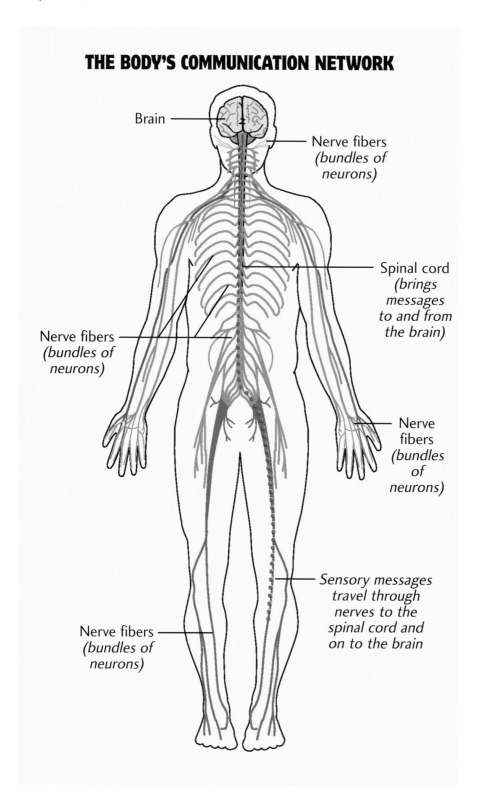

THE BODY'S COMMUNICATION NETWORK

Brain

Nerve fibers
*(bundles of
neurons)*

Spinal cord
*(brings
messages
to and from
the brain)*

Nerve fibers
*(bundles of
neurons)*

Nerve
fibers
*(bundles
of
neurons)*

*Sensory messages
travel through
nerves to the
spinal cord and
on to the brain*

Nerve fibers
*(bundles of
neurons)*

The Brain of a Genius

Was Albert Einstein the greatest thinker of all time? Many people think so. Einstein himself even wondered about his mental processes. When asked how he solved problems, he said, "Words do not seem to play any role. (There are) more or less clear images."

Einstein died in 1955. With permission from the great scientist's family, the pathologist who autopsied the body was allowed to remove and preserve the brain.

What made Einstein's intellect so superior to the rest of us? Forty years later, Sandra Witelson at McMaster University in Canada compared Einstein's brain to the 150 "normal" brains she had already studied. She found that Einstein's IPLs (inferior parietal lobes)—above the ears on both sides of the brain—were 15 percent wider than average and missing a groove found in most brains.

The IPL goes to work when a brain estimates time or speed, visualizes in three dimensions, or solves math problems. While Witelson cannot say if the large IPL made Einstein a genius, she suspects that it may indicate "connectivity or circuitry differences" that might have given him amazing intellectual powers. On the other hand, maybe that part of his brain grew because he used it so often and so well. At this point, researchers are not certain.

In humans and other animals with backbones, nerve fibers centered in the spinal cord act as a communication network. From sensory nerves in the eyes, ears, skin, and other sense organs, messages travel from all parts of the body to the brain. Other nerves carry impulses from the brain to muscles. They direct movements of all types, ranging from the most basic, such as drinking water when thirsty, to the most complex, such as sharing abstract ideas through language.

The brain also makes chemicals that carry messages and control actions. These chemicals, called hormones, travel through the bloodstream. When they reach their target organ, they bring about a change. For example, the hypothalamus in the brain directs the production of a hormone called vasopressin. This hormone, which is made by the pituitary gland, acts on the kidneys, which make urine. It prevents them from removing too much water from the blood. In this way, vasopressin helps maintain normal blood volume and pressure.

Evidence of brains in action is all around us every day.

More Brain Watching

All around you, you can see evidence of brains at work. That is because brains do much more than run bodies. They also effect many changes in the environment. For example, all animals take food, water, and oxygen from their habitats. They also leave their wastes behind. Any evidence of animal life is evidence of a brain at work.

Some changes are temporary. The songs of birds or human choirs only last for a few minutes. Other changes endure. Animal builders, for example, create structures that range from the seasonal nests of birds to huge, ornate centuries-old cathedrals that were designed and fashioned by human minds and hands.

These changes, however different, share a common source: they are all created by those amazing animal brains that are so well worth watching!

Chapter 2

The Brain in Action

Studying a brain from the outside is like looking at an office building from the street. You can judge its size, shape, and architectural details, but you cannot tell what work is being done. For that, you must go inside, where you find offices devoted to specific tasks, staff assigned to particular jobs, and employees whose only mission is to shuttle messages between offices.

Brains are much the same way. Like offices responsible for particular aspects of a business, regions of the brain are specialized. Some areas handle speech, while others manage vision, movement, decision making, and much more. In a similar fashion, some neurons specialize as messengers. Some carry sensory messages from the body to the brain. Others carry the brain's commands to the body.

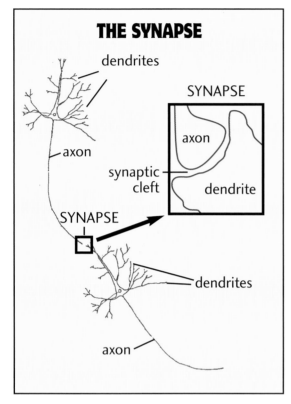

THE SYNAPSE

dendrites

axon

SYNAPSE

synaptic cleft

SYNAPSE

dendrites

axon

SYNAPSE

axon

synaptic cleft

dendrite

Signals travel along a chain of nerve cells, passing from one neuron to the next. The exchange is not direct, however, because nerve cells do not touch. Between the axon of one neuron and a dendrite of the next lies a gap called the synaptic cleft. Together, the nerve endings and the cleft form the synapse. To understand the brain in action, we must look inside to discover how signals travel along axons and cross the synapse.

The Nerve Impulse

Have you ever felt a slight electrical shock when you touched a doorknob? When your shoes slide across a carpet, electrons move from the rug into your body. Electrons are the negatively charged particles that orbit the nucleus of an atom. Gaining more electrons, your body builds up a negative charge, or potential. When you touch the doorknob, the electrons flow from you to the doorknob. The potential is discharged, and you feel a shock.

A similar process accounts for the movement of an impulse along an axon. The signal travels, not as an electrical current, but as change in potential. In a "resting neuron"—one not carrying an impulse—the charge inside a neuron is negative compared to the positive charge outside. A reversal of that difference in potential is the nerve impulse.

When channels open in the membrane (outer covering) of the neuron, positive

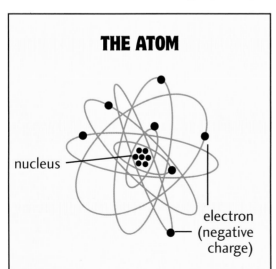

THE ATOM

nucleus

electron (negative charge)

charges rush inside. For a fraction of a second, the inside of the cell becomes more positively charged than the outside. This change in charge causes additional channels to open farther along the axon. The impulse travels from one region to the next as a wave of changing potential.

Where the impulse has passed, the neuron quickly returns to its resting state. Microscopic "pumps" inside the cell force charged atoms (called ions) out of the cell. The channels close, blocking the entry of positive charges until the next impulse comes along.

Neurotransmitters

At the tip of the axon, the comparison to shoes, carpets, and doorknobs fails. The transmission of the impulse across the synapse is chemical, not electrical. These chemical messengers are called neurotransmitters. They form in the cell body of a neuron. They move down the axon to its end, where they are stored in tiny "packets" called vesicles. When a nerve impulse reaches the tip of an axon, the membranes of the packets fuse with the cell membrane. The vesicle is then open to the outside of the cell, and its contents spill into the gap.

Molecules of neurotransmitter move across the gap, diffusing in much the same way that dye spreads through water. When they reach the membrane of a dendrite, they attach to spaces on the membrane that match their shape. These spaces are called receptors, and they fit neurotransmitter molecules precisely. The binding of the neurotransmitter to its receptor either triggers an impulse or prevents one, depending on the neurotransmitter and where it is working. The action continues until the neurotrans-

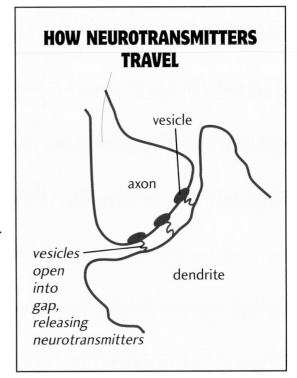

HOW NEUROTRANSMITTERS TRAVEL

vesicle

axon

vesicles open into gap, releasing neurotransmitters

dendrite

mitter molecules drift away from the receptor, break apart, or return to the axon that released them.

Neurotransmitters operate throughout the brain and nervous system. Many work at the synapse, but some operate between neurons and glial cells, diffusing in the fluid that surrounds both. Glia, once thought to be passive support structures for neurons, are now known to release the neurotransmitter glutamate and perhaps many others.

Some neurotransmitters are known, but many others may exist—perhaps 150 different kinds or more! The table on page 21 names a few and tells a little about what they do.

Stimulus and Response

Impulses travel along pathways of neurons that intersect and diverge into complex networks. Depending on which neurons and neurotransmitters are involved, the brain interprets impulses from the body as sights, sounds, tastes, smells, or touches (anything from slight pressure to intense pain). It translates impulses traveling within the brain itself into perceived ideas, thoughts, or emotions. In response to either kind of stimulus, the brain may direct the body to act in a particular way. Some such actions are involuntary.

Breathing is a good example. You seldom think about your breathing. Nevertheless, your brain is in charge. It controls breathing through a series of chemical and electric steps:
• Living cells produce the gas carbon dioxide as a waste product. The waste passes into the bloodstream.

Neurotransmitters, such as serotonin, help to regulate emotional states and promote feelings of well-being.

SOME NEUROTRANSMITTERS, THEIR FUNCTIONS, AND THEIR MISFIRES

Name	When it's working properly	When things go wrong
Serotonin	Important in controlling sleep. Promotes feelings of well-being. Helps regulate emotion.	Low levels of serotonin are associated with depression.
Acetylcholine	Causes skeletal muscles to contract but inhibits contraction of the heart muscle.	Levels are low in the brains of people with Alzheimer's disease.
Glutamate	Initiates nerve impulses. May be important in learning and memory.	Glutamate floods the brains of stroke victims and kills neurons.
GABA (gamma amino butyric acid)	Stops nerve impulses in the brain and spinal cord.	Too little makes neurons overactive and can result in seizures or epilepsy
Endorphins	Natural painkillers, released during times of extreme physical stress such as childbirth.	The addictive drug morphine docks to endorphin receptors on dendrite membranes.
Dopamine	Blocks the transmission of nerve impulses in certain areas of the brain. Involved in producing hormones, regulating movement, and storing memories.	A deficiency of dopamine causes Parkinson's disease.
Nitric oxide (a gas)	Relaxes blood vessels.	A deficiency may lead to high blood pressure.

- Carbon dioxide molecules attach to receptors in the major artery that carries blood away from the heart.
- These receptors start an impulse. It travels along a major nerve to a region in the brain stem.
- That region fires an impulse that moves along motor nerves from the brain to the muscles of the chest and diaphragm.
- The impulse causes the muscles to contract.
- Contraction expands the chest cavity and creates a difference in air pressure between the lungs and the environment. Because pressure is greater on the outside, air flows to the inside. The lungs inflate.
- Because the concentration of carbon dioxide is greater in the blood than in the air, carbon dioxide molecules diffuse out of the blood into the lungs.
- Higher in the brain stem lies another center that regulates how long a breath lasts. It shuts off the impulse that causes contraction of chest muscles.
- When the muscles relax, the chest cavity decreases in size. Air containing a load of carbon dioxide waste leaves the lungs.
- When the level of carbon dioxide rises again, the sequence repeats.

Voluntary Action

Suppose you are sitting quietly in a library, reading a book. Unconsciously, your breathing stays slow and even. Your heartbeat is gentle and regular.

Suddenly, the building begins to shake. The moving earth rattles the windows. Books begin to fall from shelves. Pencils roll off tables.

"Earthquake!" someone shouts.

Before you have time to think about what is happening, your brain reacts to the emergency with many involuntary responses.

Hey, PEA Brain! You're in Love!

Look, over there! What an attractive person! So good looking! So smart! So totally adorable!

You are in love, and the object of your love has just entered the room. It is the romantic love that poets and songwriters cannot get enough of, and who are you to argue? All you can think about is that special someone. Your palms sweat, and your stomach turns cartwheels. Before you start turning cartwheels yourself, stop and think about what love really is.

In your bloodstream, love is a tide of hormones. That flush of infatuation comes from a hormone called testosterone. Both sexes have it, although males make it in greater amounts. Its action, scientists think, accounts for that feeling of "love at first sight."

In your nervous system, love is a wave of shifting electrical potentials. Involuntary centers in the brain stem send messages to the heart and lungs. Breathing rate increases. Blood pressure rises. You may even lose control of such voluntary actions as speech when you cannot seem to utter more than a stuttering "hi."

In your brain, love is an emotional stimulus-response triggered by the action of neurotransmitters. One such neurotransmitter, dopamine, spews from a gland called the hypothalamus and targets neurons of the brain's emotional center, the limbic system. Pupils enlarge. Blood rushes to the face, causing you to blush.

Other brain chemicals get into the act, especially one called PEA (for phenylethylamine). This stimulant produces seemingly boundless enthusiasm and unlimited energy. If a new "crush" means you eat poorly or your grades slip in school, PEA is to blame. It is powerful enough to squelch appetite and erode motivation.

PEA intoxication transforms the everyday world into a magic realm of enchantment. But magic is fleeting. The brain cannot tolerate high levels of PEA for long. As the amount of PEA drops, the elation of "new love" dissolves. At this point, love is put to the test. The pair can commit to each other for a long period of companionship and mutual support. Or they can start looking for a new love and go in search of another, temporary flood of PEA.

Your brain stem accelerates your breathing. Your heart beats harder and faster. Blood pressure rises, and pupils dilate. Even the chemistry of the blood changes, making clotting easier should you be injured.

The brain enables the body to react immediately and involuntarily to emergency situations.

But the earthquake also demands some voluntary action. You cannot sit and wait this one out. You must flee! Your conscious decision to sprint for the stairs comes from your cerebral cortex. Neurons in the motor cortex signal your leg muscles to get moving—and fast! As you hurdle obstacles and dodge falling debris, your cerebellum keeps you upright and balanced. It monitors the speed, force, and direction of your movement.

As you shout the alarm to others, your brain's speech centers—located in the cortex of the left hemisphere in most people—operate at high gear. The earth trembles beneath your feet, and your stomach sinks. That is your limbic system sending the emotional signal you know as fear.

When you reach safety and the tremors cease, the flow of neurotransmitters at your synapses lessens. Neurons return to their resting state.

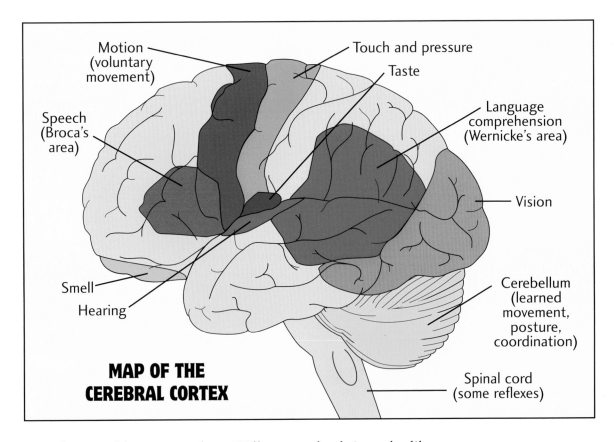

Motion (voluntary movement)
Touch and pressure
Taste
Language comprehension (Wernicke's area)
Speech (Broca's area)
Vision
Smell
Hearing
Cerebellum (learned movement, posture, coordination)
Spinal cord (some reflexes)

MAP OF THE CEREBRAL CORTEX

Breathing and heart rate slow. Will you go back into the library to retrieve your book? Whatever the answer, it will come from brain centers that lie toward the top and front of your cerebral cortex. These regions form purpose, shape plans, and exercise judgment.

In the days that follow, no one will be able to look at you and tell that you survived an earthquake. But you will know. Just as businesses keep records, your "office building" of a brain maintains an archive you call memory. Everything you have ever done—everything that has ever happened to you— is stored there.

Chapter **3**

Specializing

Until the 1970s, scientists had no way to look inside the living brain. They learned from people whose brains were damaged by injury or illness. For example, Canadian doctors worked with a woman who had a serious injury to the back of her brain. She had no trouble reaching out and grasping a rectangular block, but she could not tell whether it was sitting horizontally or vertically on a table.

Such examples show that different areas of the brain do different jobs. One function can be lost, while others remain normal. Today, scientists use PET and MRI pictures (see page 30) to pinpoint sites of brain action. From such images, they learn how the "average" human brain works and how individual people differ.

Hemispheres

Everyone's brain is different, but the basic map is the same for all humans. For example, the regions of the cerebral cortex that control movement operate opposite sides of the body. The left brain manages the right side and vice versa. That explains why people who have strokes often experience paralysis on one side of the body but not the other.

The hemispheres also specialize in mental tasks. They differ not so much in what they do as in how they do it. The left brain handles information in sequence. That's good for words that come one at a time, with an order that has meaning. In most people, speech and language are handled mostly by the left hemisphere. The right brain organizes fragments of information into a complete pattern. That is the best way to recognize faces, get from one place to another, and solve problems involving spatial relationships.

The hemispheres do not work alone. They continuously communicate across the bundle of nerve fibers called the corpus callosum. Despite their specialties, both hemispheres participate whether an activity is "logical" or "creative." For example, researchers at Johns Hopkins University found that—in times of stress—the left brain analyzes choices while the right brain worries. Rather than being a hindrance, the worrying plays an important role. It lets emotions steer decision making toward options that are right, moral, and fair.

The specialties of the hemispheres are neither fixed nor permanent, at least in some cases. Pennsylvania researchers studied people who survived stroke damage to the left hemisphere's speech centers. As the patients recovered, their

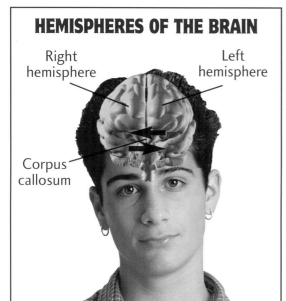

HEMISPHERES OF THE BRAIN

Right hemisphere

Left hemisphere

Corpus callosum

right hemispheres took over some language functions. Their speech improved as their brains rewired and reorganized.

The Lobes

Brain maps show how hemispheres specialize. They also show the division of labor among the lobes of the cerebral cortex:

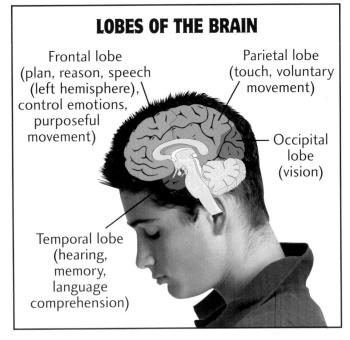

LOBES OF THE BRAIN

Frontal lobe (plan, reason, speech (left hemisphere), control emotions, purposeful movement)

Parietal lobe (touch, voluntary movement)

Occipital lobe (vision)

Temporal lobe (hearing, memory, language comprehension)

- The parietal lobes at the top of the head receive information from the sense of touch. The motor cortex in front of the parietal lobes controls voluntary movement.

- The temporal lobes lie at the sides of the head above the ears. An area of the temporal lobe called the auditory cortex processes nerve impulses from the ears. In about 90 percent of right-handed people and 70 percent of left-handed people, the centers for understanding spoken language lie in the left temporal lobe.

- The occipital lobes lie at the back of the head just above the cerebellum. They interpret input from the eyes. This area is often called the visual cortex.

- The frontal lobes lie just behind the forehead. They manage new situations and comprehend complex ideas. They reason, plan, and control emotions. They also direct the motor cortex to carry out purposeful movement.

Memory

Although many brain functions have been traced to certain regions, memory is not localized (though key memory systems are located in the temporal lobe). In a sense, memories are

Pictures Inside the Brain

When a brain area goes to work, it uses more oxygen and sugar (food) than other areas. Two procedures that detect the differences allow scientists to take pictures of activity inside the living brain.

One technique is functional magnetic resonance imaging, or MRI. In the magnetic field generated by the MRI scanner, hydrogen atoms in the body's water molecules vibrate. They emit weak radio signals that computers can read as pictures.

The other method is positron emission tomography, abbreviated PET. Radioactive forms of elements serve as "tracers." Oxygen atoms (in water) or carbon atoms (in sugar) are often used. As they travel through the body, tracer atoms emit positively charged particles, or positrons. When positrons collide with electrons, they give off gamma rays. PET equipment detects the gamma rays, and a computer converts them into colored pictures.

Brain images are important in both medicine and research. PET and MRI help surgeons locate and remove brain tumors. Physicians use them to treat people with epilepsy and head injuries. Researchers study healthy brains to learn how we think, feel, and remember. Much of our knowledge about how brain areas specialize comes from PET and MRI studies.

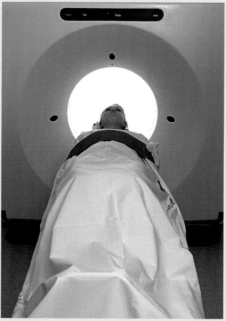

People are often completely surrounded by an MRI machine.

everywhere in the brain. Stimulation of a specific area in the brain may bring back a vivid memory, such as a favorite game from childhood or the smell of gardenias. However, damage to that area will not always destroy that memory.

Trauma—either physical or psychological—can wipe out some memories but not others. For example, a person with temporary amnesia may forget what happened in the moments before an accident, while memory of the distant past remains clear.

Memories are fixed, most scientists think, when pathways between neurons grow stronger. If a signal passes from an axon to a dendrite once, it is more likely to do so again. Exactly how such pathways are built and preserved is the subject of much research.

Scientists know more about how memories are stored than about where. Two parts of the limbic system—the hippocampus and the amygdala—are especially important. They link emotion to experience. Perhaps that explains why people remember best those things they felt strongly about.

The brain integrates many elements— such as knowledge, memory, emotion, and movement—in order to respond to a physical need like hunger.

Cooperation

Specialization does not mean that brain centers operate independently. The brain integrates feelings, knowledge, memory, and movement. For example, when the brain receives signals from an empty stomach, it recognizes hunger and concludes that food will stop the pangs. It retrieves memories of good things to eat. It recalls where and how to find and prepare food. These sensations and memories trigger both conscious decision and physical action. Early in human history, they sent hunter-gatherers in search of berries and bison. Today, they send consumers dashing to food stores and restaurants. In either case, brain regions work together in making plans and carrying them through.

More to Learn

Each year, PET and MRI pictures reveal more about the brain's inner workings. Scientists want to know, for example, how the brain processes spatial information. Scans show that certain parts of the brain recognize and identify shapes, while other parts mentally manipulate or rotate them.

Scientists in Los Angeles took MRI pictures while people tried to solve shape comparison and rotation problems by visualizing the answers in their heads. In most of their subjects, brain activity increased in the parietal lobes, the visual centers, and an area that concentrates attention on difficult tasks. The scientists were surprised to find that many subjects also showed increased activity in the areas that detect motion. They suspect that the brain may handle information on real and imagined motion as if they were the same.

People varied greatly in the brain regions they used to solve these problems. For example, if a puzzle (like the one below) permits either a verbal or a spatial solution, individual brains will probably choose one over the other. The more skill people develop in their preferred strategies, the less energy the relevant brain areas use. Is the brain lazy? No, just efficient.

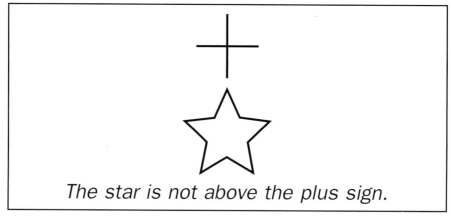

The star is not above the plus sign.

Is the statement above true or false? Some people answer by processing visual images. Other people use words.

Learning from Mistakes?

Scientists at the University of Iowa think they have found the area of the brain that allows people to learn from their mistakes.

They studied two people whose brains were damaged early in life. One was run over by a car at age 15 months. The other had a brain tumor removed in infancy. Both recovered physically and developed normally as young children, but troubles appeared later. One ran away from home, lied, shoplifted, and had trouble with social relationships. The other overate, stole, and attacked people. Neither could hold a job or plan for the future. They showed no remorse for the harm they caused others.

On tests of moral reasoning, these people could not distinguish right from wrong. Using MRI to look inside their brains, scientists found damage to the one or both frontal lobes. These brain areas, researchers concluded, must be important to learning from mistakes.

Adults injured in those brain areas become impulsive and socially awkward, but they know right from wrong. These two, injured in childhood, never developed moral knowledge. They were not breaking the rules on purpose, says Iowa brain scientist Antonio Damasio. They simply could not learn them. The rewards and punishments that shape social behavior had no effect on their damaged brains. Researchers have also begun to study this information as it applies to criminals and antisocial behavior. Some researchers believe that certain criminals may have some form of frontal lobe damage.

Chapter 4

Communicating

Which of the following words rhyme: show, shoe, how, roe? If you are like most people, speech centers behind your left eyebrow told you that show and roe sound the same. If you are female, you may have used a center behind your right eyebrow as well.

Name something that flies. If you said bird, airplane, or astronaut, activity increased in several areas of your cortex. The brain centers that recall the names of animals, objects, or people differ from those that handle the sounds of speech, such as rhymes.

Speaking and Understanding

Many experts think that knowledge of grammar and syntax is "hardwired" into the human brain at birth. Every language has nouns, verbs, and adjectives. The brain categorizes and relates them, no matter what language is learned.

Scientists used to think the brain used only two areas for all its language processing. One is called Broca's area, named for the French surgeon who discovered it. In 1864, Pierre Peter Broca offered evidence that a region in the left frontal lobe controls speech. Broca's area lies close to motor areas that cause the mouth, lips, tongue, and larynx to form the sounds of words. People with damage in Broca's area lose all or part of their ability to speak.

The second language center is called Wernicke's area, named for the German doctor who discovered it. This area lies in the left temporal lobe. There, the brain gets meaning from words and sentences. A person with damage in this area cannot understand language.

Today we know that several other brain regions work together with Broca's and Wernicke's areas. For example, a part of the temporal lobe supplies nouns, such as airplane, bird, and astronaut. Another supplies verbs, such as fly, take off, and orbit. Yet another puts the two together. The result is the potential for billions of complete sentences. Birds fly. Airplanes take off. Astronauts orbit. Think of a blue bird, a 747 airplane, or a Russian cosmonaut, and still other centers get into the act.

One Brain, Many Languages

Humans think without language. People who neither hear nor speak still plan, daydream, remember, and make choices—all without words. Some learn sign language and it works just as well as spoken language. It is processed in the same areas of the left hemisphere as speech, although it uses movements instead of

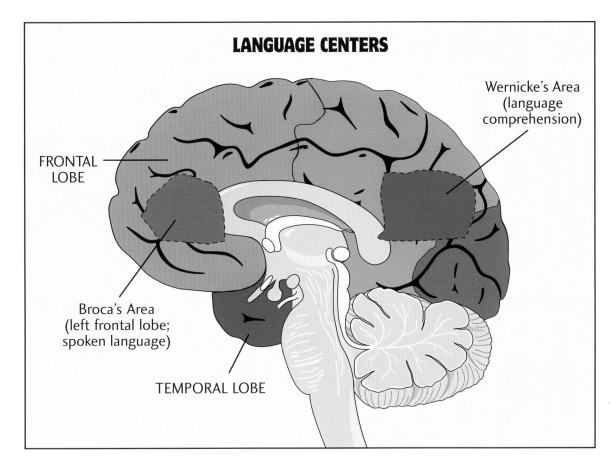

LANGUAGE CENTERS

Wernicke's Area (language comprehension)

FRONTAL LOBE

Broca's Area (left frontal lobe; spoken language)

TEMPORAL LOBE

sounds to communicate meaning. People who learned sign language in childhood, whether hearing or deaf, use the corresponding areas of the right hemisphere in addition to the left hemisphere speech centers.

What about people who master two or more languages? George Ojemann at the University of Washington studied bilingual people. In one, he found neurons that fired to speak Finnish, but not English. In another, he found cells that processed English but not Spanish. Bilingual people store knowledge of their native language differently than their second language—if they learn it later in life. If learned in childhood, both languages are processed through the same brain centers.

Learning a language, then, influences which brain areas process speech and how they specialize. From such observations, scientists draw a general conclusion. The brain develops differently depending on the inputs it receives.

Reading

Do you recall "see it, say it, read it?" Teachers help beginning readers to associate the sound of a word with its appearance in writing. Good readers can mentally convert a written word to its sound in less than 0.04 seconds (four hundredths of a second). Poor readers may need 0.5 seconds (one half-second). Their slow auditory processing interferes with reading, although they have no trouble with speech.

Reading is, however, more complicated than "see and say." PET and MRI studies show that the brain does not need to sound out a written word to get meaning from it. Visual centers send signals directly to Wernicke's area where the word is understood without sound—real or imagined. If the brain's visual centers cannot recognize words fast enough, reading is difficult.

Nearly three of every four deaf people who read English do not process the written word in the brain's left hemisphere as most hearing people do. Instead, MRI pictures show activity in parts of the right parietal and temporal lobes where spatial relationships are handled. People blind from birth who learn to read Braille show activity in the brain's visual centers when they read—even though they have never seen the Braille characters. The brain, it seems, does not need eyes to form pictures, or ears to capture words.

While reading, visual centers in the brain send signals to Wernicke's area, where each word is understood without an accompanying sound.

Can Aliens Communicate?

"Men are from Mars and women are from Venus," claims author John Gray in his best-selling book. His point is that men and women speak in such different ways, they have as much trouble under-standing each other as would aliens from different planets. Do brain scientists agree? Not totally, but male and female brains do differ in how they handle language.

On the average, females are more verbal than males. Girls talk earlier, read more easily, and win word games more often. On elementary school reading tests, the average girl outscores the average boy in spelling, grammar, vocabulary, and comprehension. In later life, women who recover from strokes and brain injuries are more likely than men to regain their language abilities—and to do so more quickly.

PET and MRI pictures suggest some reasons why. In general, male brains are more specialized. Their left and right hemispheres work independently on many tasks. Women's brains typically use both sides at the same time. For example, when asked to sing a song and lift a finger for each four-letter word, both male and female brains work in a small region on the left side. In addition, women use areas on the right side, including visual centers. Is it possible that women form a mental image of the word and men do not?

In women, the frontal lobes of the brain play a greater role in language comprehension. Some studies suggest that women's brains, though smaller than men's, contain about 11 percent more neurons. The extra nerve cells are packed into the layers of the cortex that understand language, recognize melodies, and distinguish tones of voice.

Does this mean that boys cannot read, write, or spell? Not at all. "It's easy to find....men who excel in language skills," says Johns Hopkins scientist Godfrey Pearlson. "Only when we look at very large populations and look for slight but significant trends do we see generalizations."

More important, individuals of the same sex differ more than the average difference between the sexes. That's good news for "Martians" and "Venusians," because it suggests that a man and a woman have as good a chance of under-standing each other as do any two women or two men. Earthlings can communicate without a Martian-Venusian dictionary, but careful listening and thoughtful speaking are essential.

How Does the Brain Put It All Together?

How does information from different brain centers come together? University of Iowa scientist Antonio Damasio studied a man he called Boswell. Boswell had an infection that damaged some of his brain, but he could speak and understand most language. His loss came in connecting words and ideas. For example, he could say "California" in response to "Los Angeles," but when asked to name a city in California, he could not. Boswell also lost the ability to recognize faces. Tests showed that his brain reacted differently to familiar and unfamiliar faces, but he could not state with words that he knew the difference. Boswell lost, according to Damasio, not the information, but the ability to access it.

Normal brains can experience problems with bringing ideas together. To see for yourself, do this: Cover the right-hand column below with your hand and read the words in the left-hand column. Easy, right? Now uncover the right-hand column and read those words. Were you slow? Was the list confusing? This phenomenon is called interference. Your brain—when presented with color words different from the colors seen—does not know which processing loop to use. You can consciously "force" your brain circuits to attend to the words and ignore the colors, but not easily.

YELLOW	YELLOW
GREEN	GREEN
BLUE	BLUE
RED	RED
ORANGE	ORANGE

This brain teaser is called the Stroop Color Test. Brain areas interfere with each other when words and colors don't match.

Mind Reading

Most human beings can read the minds of others to some degree. Gestures, body posture, and tone of voice reveal thoughts more clearly than words ever could. For example, say aloud the sentence "You're late," as:

1. a statement of trivial fact—true, but not important.
2. an accusation.
3. a command to spur someone to hurry.

In each instance, the words are the same, but the meaning is different. Body language would be just as important as tone of voice in helping you comprehend the difference. Match the following to the situations above.

A. Stance tall, feet planted wide, hands on hips, eyes blazing.
B. Soft tone, scarcely glancing up from a newspaper.
C. Waving wildly and pointing toward the distance.

If you matched 1-B, 2-A, and 3-C, you are probably as good a mind reader as most.

Unfortunately, some people cannot "read" the tones and gestures of others. Many autistic children experience such "mindblindness." Trapped in a world of their own, they cannot tell what others think, feel, or want. They do not experience embarrassment or pride, because they do not understand that people have opinions about one another. They cannot infer the mental reasons why people act as they do. For example, you probably know why a parent would shout, "You're late!" The parent is worried, irritated, angry, or disappointed—depending on the tone. But a "mindblind" person has no idea about a reason. Understanding that others have a "state of mind" is incomprehensible.

Simon Baron-Cohen, who coined the term "mindblindness," says most people "mindread all the time, effortlessly, automatically, and mostly unconsciously." He thinks mindreading is a necessity. "Without it," he says, "human society as we know it simply would not exist."

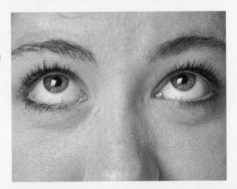

Growing and Changing

The brain you have today is not the brain you had yesterday. It is not the brain you will have tomorrow. The human brain changes continuously throughout life.

Before Birth

All the body's tissues, organs, and systems arise from the fertilized egg. The single cell divides, becoming 2, 4, 8, 16, and so on, until the hollow ball of cells pushes inward forming two cell layers. Later, it will become three.

By the sixteenth day after fertilization, part of the embryo's outer cell layer has thickened in the middle. At this thickening, the neural plate becomes visible. In the next few days, it forms twin, parallel sides that fold inward, becoming the open neural groove. The closing of the groove forms the neural tube.

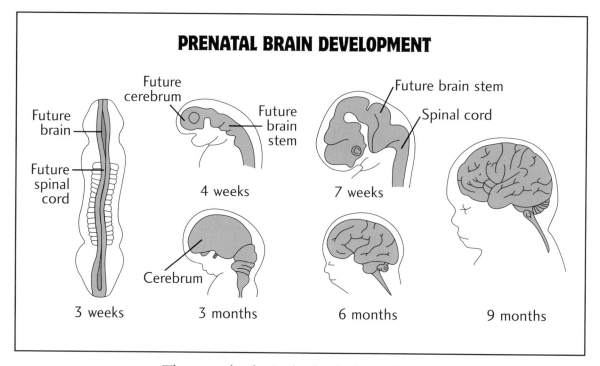

PRENATAL BRAIN DEVELOPMENT

Future brain
Future spinal cord
3 weeks

Future cerebrum
Future brain stem
4 weeks

Cerebrum
3 months

Future brain stem
Spinal cord
7 weeks

6 months

9 months

The neural tube is the birthplace of neurons. From there, neurons migrate along pathways of "guide cells." Guide cells make attractant and repellent chemicals that act as chemical "traffic controllers." They steer neurons into three bulges at the front of the neural tube. These bulges become the brain stem, limbic system, and cerebrum. Cells along the outer edges of the tube grow away from it. They become the nerves that connect the brain and spinal cord to the rest of the body.

In the fourth and fifth months of fetal development, axons and dendrites grow close enough together to form synapses. Transmission of nerve impulses along simple pathways becomes possible.

The fetus develops inside the mother's uterus, floating in a sac of fluids. The chemistry of the internal environment affects brain growth and development. If the mother drinks alcohol, smokes, takes drugs, or eats poorly, she risks injury to her child's brain and nervous system.

Infancy and Childhood

Some of the brain's functions operate at birth. For example, newborns reveal through their eye movements that they can do simple arithmetic, although they cannot speak or write. They respond to their mother's language more than to a foreign language. They also respond to music that was played before they were born. Those findings suggest that the fetus processes nerve impulses before birth.

In the first year after birth, the production of neurons slows, but the number of connections among them increases rapidly. Connections result from everything the infant sees, hears, tastes, touches, or smells. The neurons used most often begin to form networks. Those that are not used are discarded.

The development of sight is a good example of how the process works. At birth, visual neurons process input from both eyes. As the baby grows, some of those neurons specialize in accepting signals from one eye only. Anything that interferes with input

Recent studies have shown that a newborn's brain is more complex than previously thought.

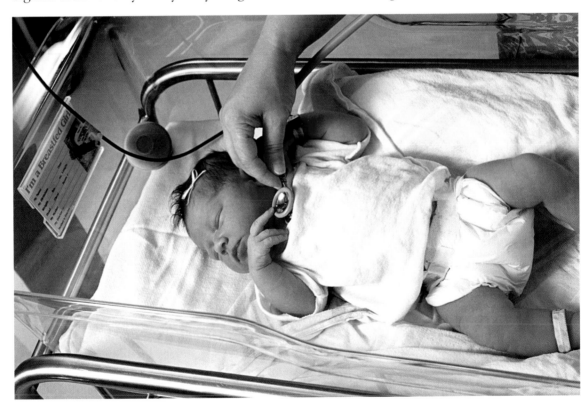

Between the ages of three and eight, a human brain has twice the number of neural connections it will have in adulthood.

from the right or left eye, such as an eye patch or a cataract, can cause "brain blindness" due to atrophied neurons. Even if the eye develops normally, the visual centers of the brain do not.

Between ages 3 and 8, a child's brain has twice as many neurons as it will have in adulthood. It uses twice as much energy and can form about four times as many connections. Learning is faster and easier in childhood than it will be later. This is the best time to learn languages, play a musical instrument, or master a sport.

Researchers at UCLA studied the brains of normal children from age three into their teen years. In those between ages 3 and 6, they saw rapid growth spurts in brain areas that plan and organize action and direct attention to a task. Between the ages of 6 and 12, growth was greatest in language and math areas in the brain.

The Teen Years

As sexual maturity approaches (usually around age 11 in girls and 12 in boys), the front part of the brain produces a large number of immature connections between neurons. These connections are not yet "wired" into neural pathways, but are

MAJOR GROWTH OF BRAIN TISSUE

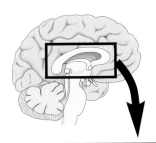

These illlustrations show which areas of the human brain experience the most concentrated growth between the ages of 3-13. The growth is highlighted in the corpus callosum, the major fiber tract that relays information between the left and right hemispheres.

Ages 3-6
Frontal region
(planning and paying attention)

Ages 6-7
Mid region
(supports mathematical thinking)

Ages 8-13
Rear region
(language and spatial areas)

available for use as needed. They are still changing substantially and new connections are made that grow stronger the more they are used. Because they have a greater ability to make connections, teens can learn in an hour what might take an adult much longer.

Over time, the total numbers of connections increase in some areas of the brain and decrease in others. Researchers have found, for example, a loss of connections in the frontal lobes during the mid-teens. The frontal lobes regulate emotion and control impulses. Some researchers wonder if the loss of connections there has anything to do with the moodiness and unpredictable behavior that perplex the parents of many teens.

"Pruning" is rapid in the teen years. Unused connections are discarded, sometimes at the rate of thousands a second. Only those that are strengthened by experience survive. The result is fewer connections, presumably operating more efficiently.

The brain makes chemicals that affect the body in adolescence. The hypothalamus releases high levels of a chemical that stimulates appetite. Body weight increases. That supports growth in boys and provides girls with the stored energy their bodies need to support the menstrual cycle or pregnancy.

Hormones made in the maturing sex organs affect the brain. In girls, the hippocampus responds to female hormones and grows faster than in boys. In boys, male hormones cause the amygdala to grow faster than in girls.

In both sexes, development of different brain areas occurs at different times. By age 12, the sensory and language pathways are well established, but the parts of the parietal lobe that integrate data from the senses are still maturing well into the mid-teens. The regions of purposeful action and emotional control in the frontal lobes reach their maximum size at about age 16. Only then do they begin pruning and becoming more efficient.

Jay Giedd, a researcher at the National Institute of Mental Health in Bethesda, Maryland, says that children have little control over their brain development, but teens have a great deal. "Use it or lose it," he advises. Reading, sports, travel, social experiences, and hobbies—all contribute to active brain development in the teen years. (Watching television does not.) School is important, too. A college student may develop as many as 40 percent more connections among neurons than a high school dropout.

At the onset of adolescence, the front part of the brain produces a large number of new connections. This provides potential for learning many new things.

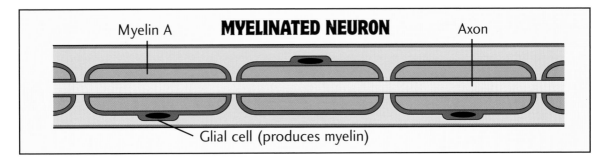

MYELINATED NEURON

Myelin A   Axon

Glial cell (produces myelin)

Adulthood

Although the brain reaches 95 percent of its adult size by age 5, it continues to renew, reshape, and reorganize itself throughout life. Thousands of new cells are created daily, especially in the hippocampus, where memories of faces and places are formed. New cells also arise in the cerebral cortex in the areas of thought and personality.

Myelin coats the axons of neurons, making them more efficient at sending messages quickly.

The brain grows more efficient in adult life. From the late teens into the twenties, pruning continues, eliminating unused connections. Also, myelin, a fatty insulating substance, continues to grow around axons. Myelin protects axons and increases the speed of the traveling impulse. The corpus callosum grows in adult life, too, possibly improving the communication between left and right hemispheres.

Specialized brain areas become fully functional in adulthood. For example, teens often fail to read the emotions underlying facial expressions. Adults nearly always succeed. They know anger and joy and fear when they see it. In adult life, judgment expands. Making careful decisions becomes both more likely and more comfortable.

Learning is as important in adult life as it was earlier. The more the brain is used, the greater the number of connections between neurons, and the stronger they become. No one knows exactly what strengthens a connection, but some scientists think the physical structure and chemical communication of the synapse may change.

Walk Yourself Smart

Want to get smarter? Try walking!

That is the advice of researchers at the University of Illinois who studied 100 previously inactive adults between the ages of 60 to 75. Some of the women and men in the study started walking three times a week. Some did stretching and toning exercises.

The scientists used computer tasks to test their subjects' mental sharpness. They measured their ability to switch from one task to another, focus on a task while ignoring distractions, and stop an activity quickly.

After 6 months, the walkers scored as much as 15 percent higher than the stretchers and toners. The scientists think the improvements may come from increasing the brain's oxygen supply.

Exercise causes chemical changes in the brain that boost learning. In mice, exercise increases the number of neurons in the hippocampus, where memories form. Does the same thing happen in people? Maybe. It's possible that neurotransmitters, growth factors, or higher oxygen levels might stimulate the production of neurons.

Although less so than in childhood, the adult brain can "rewire" itself after an injury. For example, when a blockage in a blood vessel cuts off their supply of oxygen, brain cells die. That is one kind of stroke. Strokes often paralyze one side of the body, or one part such as a leg, hand, or arm. Usually, damage to the brain's left side paralyzes the body's right side and vice versa.

However, many people who have strokes regain total or partial movement, especially if they participate in rehabilitation therapy. MRI pictures show what happens during recovery. For a while, the brain on the same side as the paralysis becomes active as the person tries to move the paralyzed muscles. As motion improves, the side where the stroke occurred begins to take back control. It seems the opposite side "helps out" until the injured side either forms new connections or drafts formerly unused ones into service.

Old Age

As the brain ages, it shrinks in size—more in the frontal lobes than elsewhere. Individual axons and dendrites shrink, too. Blood flow and energy use in the cerebral cortex lessen. The brain produces less of the nerve growth factor, NGF, that makes dendrites branch and grow. Despite the overall shrinkage, certain areas of the brain, such as the fluid-filled ventricles, actually enlarge.

The neurotransmitter acetylcholine is very important to

As the human body ages, the brain shrinks in size.

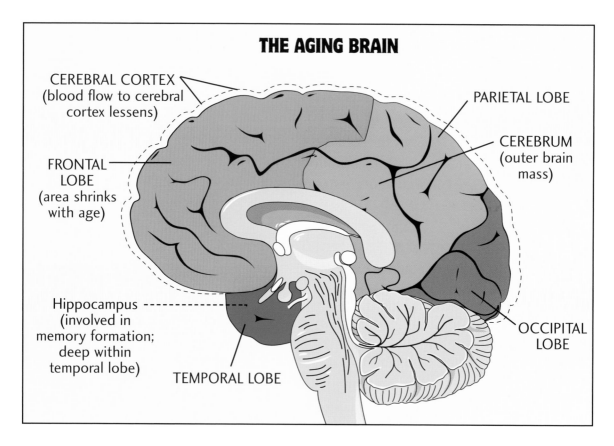

THE AGING BRAIN

CEREBRAL CORTEX
(blood flow to cerebral
cortex lessens)

PARIETAL LOBE

CEREBRUM
(outer brain
mass)

FRONTAL
LOBE
(area shrinks
with age)

Hippocampus
(involved in
memory formation;
deep within
temporal lobe)

OCCIPITAL
LOBE

TEMPORAL LOBE

memory. Its production declines in old age, but new brain cells may help compensate for the loss. Researchers at the Salk Institute in California found that the brains of elderly patients produce between 500 and 1,000 new brain cells every day. Most of the cells do not mature fully, but those in the hippocampus do. The hippocampus is important to learning and memory.

The brain can also call other pathways into action when existing circuits break down. Remembering visual images is one ability that stays sharp well into old age. However, the elderly use different parts of the brain for short-term visual memory than young adults do.

Although declines in memory are typical among the elderly, the loss is significant in no more than 10 percent of those over 65 and perhaps 20 percent of those older than 85. Nearly a

third of people in their 80s do mental arithmetic as well as young adults do. Older people do better than young ones on tests of judgment and decision making. It is true that wisdom comes with age.

Those who stay mentally fit in old age kept mentally fit when they were young. They are typically well educated, enjoy many and varied activities, and interact with people as smart and interesting as they are. Using neurons increases the number of dendrites and the number of connections among neurons well into old age.

Elderly people that keep both their bodies and their minds fit stand a better chance of keeping their brain functions sharp.

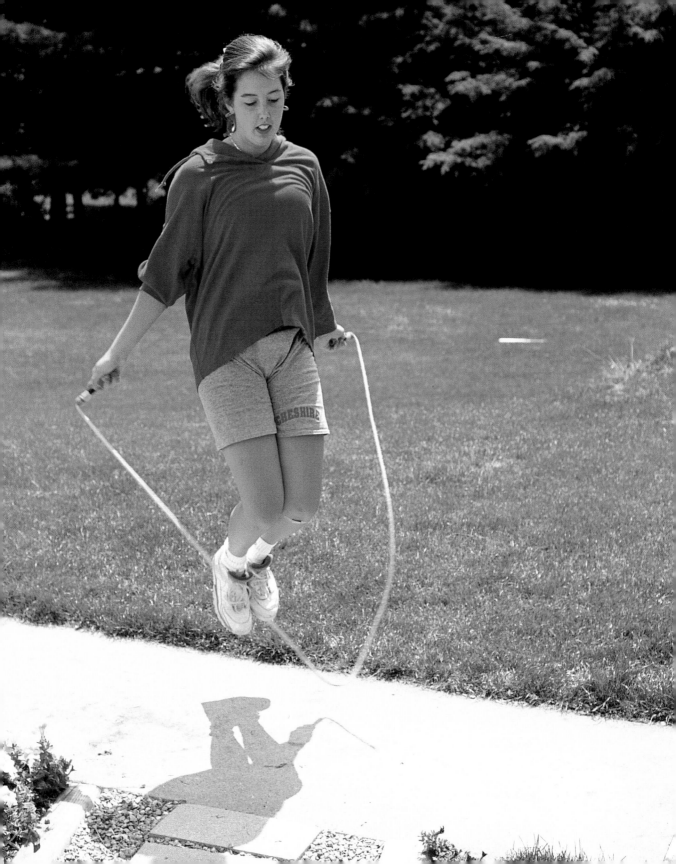

6

Marvel and Mystery

What weighs three pounds, looks like a cauliflower, and wants to understand itself? The human brain!

If you have been brain watching lately, perhaps you have noticed how well brains work. People open their mouths and their thoughts come out in language. It happens without effort, it seems, and only rarely is an idea lost or a word misspoken. Have you noticed brains directing other activities? People walk, run, swim, jump, sing, read, write, and imagine—all because of a three-pound organ cradled inside their skulls.

Since 1990, scientists have learned more about the human brain than was discovered in all the centuries before. Yet, we still know very little. So much remains to be learned about this marvel and mystery.

Medicine

One of the reasons for research on the brain is the hope of helping people who have diseases. Parkinson's disease is one example. It usually strikes people older than 50, although it can begin in younger adults. It causes trembling, stiffness of the shoulders and back, and difficulty walking. Parkinson's happens because of the death of neurons that produce the neurotransmitter dopamine. When these neurons die, dopamine levels fall. Drugs that raise dopamine levels help, but better treatments—and perhaps a cure—are the goals of research.

Research on nerve growth factor (NGF) offers hope for people whose spinal cords are injured in accidents. Normally, nerves do not regrow and repair themselves the way skin, muscles, and bones do. If ways could be found to stimulate nerve growth, people paralyzed by strokes or accidents might be able to walk again.

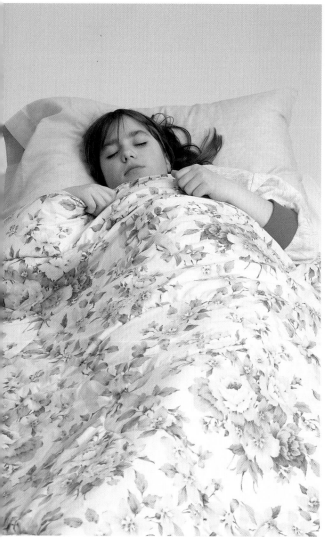

There is much data about sleep, but the purpose of sleep for the brain has yet to be determined.

Life and Living

Not all brain research seeks to cure disease or heal injuries. Much of the knowledge scientists seek can be applied to everyday life. Sleep research offers a good example. The need for sleep is obvious. Try going a few days without it! Yet no one knows why we sleep or what purpose sleep serves in the brain. Some research points to sleep, especially dreaming, as essential to learning. Why? How? Is that sleep's only function? Those questions remain unanswered.

Many other mysteries await solution. How do our brains keep time so that we sleep at night, work in the day, and adjust our body clocks when we jet across time zones? How do our senses work? How does the brain integrate knowledge from all the senses into the coherent experience we call reality? What is intelligence? Can we get smarter by eating right, exercising, or taking a "smart pill?" What about physical activity? Are there better ways to learn to pole vault or train for the Olympic decathlon?

Technology

Sometimes, people compare the human brain to a computer, but the brain is far superior. It never becomes obsolete. It can renew and reorganize itself to meet a new challenge, and its owner is never aware of the redesign. Amazingly, a healthy brain can repair itself when injured. It requires little maintenance and no service calls. Its "hard drive" capacity can never be exceeded. What's more, it lasts a lifetime.

Some scientists imagine a time when those things will be true of "thinking machines." If neural networks like those in the human brain can be made to grow and work in computers, who knows what technology might achieve?

Researchers are still studying the connection between physical achievement and brain function.

Brain Clocks, Body Clocks

Are you a lark or a night owl? Larks feel their best in the morning. They awake eager to face the day. Night owls cannot seem to function until noon. When are their best work times? In the evening or the wee small hours of the morning.

For both larks and owls, the brain serves as the master timekeeper. It controls everything from normal fluctuations in body temperature to the afternoon slump that invites a nap. But how does this clock work?

Scientists at the Scripps Institute in La Jolla, California, turned to fruit fly brains to research this question. They already knew that some kind of brain clock was involved. Normal fruit flies hatch from their pupal cases in the morning, but those with damaged brains can hatch at any time of the day.

The Scripps scientists studied fruit fly brains using techniques that let them see protein molecules in living cells. They tracked a protein called PER. They found that PER production switches on and off to establish the body's daily rhythms. They found also that PER production has highs and lows in many other organs and tissues. The brain, it seems, is not the body's only clock.

These findings raise another question. Body clocks can be reset by light—ask any international traveler—so body clocks, as well as brain clocks, must respond to light. Cells in the retina of the eye (different from visual cells) sense light and send messages to the brain's clock. But how do other body clocks detect light? No one knows, but blue-light sensitive proteins found deep within body tissues may hold the answer.

Cosmic Questions

Finally, scientists are beginning to tackle, as never before, the questions once considered the domain of philosophers. How does the physical structure of the brain create that sense of self and experience that we call the mind? What is consciousness? How do we come to understand ourselves as a part of the world around us? Can that three-pound organ that seeks to understand itself succeed?

Keep brain watching, and maybe you will find out.

Even though every human brain is constructed the same way, each produces a unique human being with a unique sense of self.

Glossary

Amygdala A part of the limbic system in the human brain associated with the formation of new memories. *See also* hippocampus.

Atom The smallest part into which an element can be divided; consists of one or more electrons orbiting a nucleus that may contain one or more protons and neutrons.

Axon The long, thin strand that carries impulses away from the cell body of a neuron.

Blood-brain barrier A network of tightly-packed cells of the brain's blood vessels that prevents the passage of many harmful substances from the blood into the brain.

Brain stem The area at the base of the brain that controls many basic life functions such as heartbeat and breathing.

Broca's area The area of the brain, usually in the left frontal lobe, that controls the production of speech.

Cerebellum The area of the brain that controls many aspects of movement, including balance and learned skills.

Cerebrum The majority of the human brain, divided by a fissure into the right and left hemispheres.

Cortex In humans, the thin outer layer of the cerebrum responsible for most higher-level thought and sensory perception.

Dendrite A thin branch typically shorter than an axon that carries impulses toward the cell body of a neuron.

Electron A negatively charged subatomic particle that orbits the nucleus of an atom.

Frontal lobes Brain areas at the front of the head, behind the forehead of the skull.

Glia or glial cells In the brain, cells that support neurons and play a role in impulse transmission and brain repair.

Hemisphere Either the left or the right side of the cerebrum.

Hippocampus A part of the limbic system in the human brain associated with the formation of new memories. *See also* amygdala.

Hormone A chemical secreted from one organ that travels through the bloodstream to another organ, where it produces some effect.

Hypothalamus A part of the brain that coordinates the nervous system, controls life processes, and helps to oversee emotions.

Impulse A wave of changing electrical potential that travels along the axons and dendrites of neurons.

Interference The tendency of two or more competing brain functions to hinder one another.

Limbic system Several structures inside the brain, including the amygdala, thalamus, corpus callosum, hippocampus, and olfactory bulb, that control some basic life functions, manage emotions, and promote formation of new memories.

Mindblindness The inability of some people with autism and other brain abnormalities to read the mental states of others from tones and gestures.

Motor neuron A neuron that carries an impulse from the brain or spinal cord to a muscle, where it stimulates contraction.

MRI (Magnetic Resonance Imaging) A technique for imaging the brain and other internal organs using the radio signals emitted by hydrogen atoms vibrating in a magnetic field.

Myelin A protective covering of protein and fat that surrounds axons and speeds impulse transmission in some neurons.

Nerve cell *See* neuron.

Nerve fiber Any one of the many bundles of neurons that link the brain and spinal cord with the rest of the body.

Nerve impulse *See* impulse.

Neural groove The open, U-shaped structure that results from the infolding of the sides of the neural plate during embryo development.

Neural plate A thickening in the early embryo that develops into the brain and nervous system.

Neural tube The tube that results from the closure of the neural groove in the embryo. Bulges at the head end of the neural tube develop into the brain. Neurons form in the neural tube.

Neuron A cell that carries the nerve impulse, consisting of a cell body, and axon, and many dendrites.

Neurotransmitter Any one of 150 or more chemicals released from an axon that crosses the synaptic cleft and initiates an impulse in another neuron; more generally, any naturally produced chemical that affects the action of the brain or nervous system.

NGF (Nerve Growth Factor) A hormone that promotes an increase in the size or number of nerve cells.

Occipital lobes Brain regions at the back of the head.

Parietal lobes Brain regions at the crown of the head.

PET (Positron Emission Tomography) A method of imaging the brain and other internal organs using radioactive tracers to identify regions of increased glucose or oxygen use.

Pruning The elimination of synaptic connections that are not used.

Receptor (dendrite) A site on the dendrite that accepts and binds a neurotransmitter released from an axon.

Resting neuron A neuron not carrying an impulse. (*See* impulse)

Sensory neuron A nerve cell that carries an impulse from a sense organ to the brain or spinal cord.

Stroke The death of brain cells, which may be caused by blockage of the blood supply or by bleeding in the brain.

Synapse Collectively, the end of one axon, a synaptic cleft, and the end of a dendrite.

Synaptic cleft The space between the axon of one neuron and a dendrite of another.

Temporal lobes The brain regions at the side of the head, above the ears.

Wernicke's area The area of the brain that controls comprehension of language.

For More Information

Books

Ballard, Carol. *How Do We Think?* Austin, TX: Steck-Vaughn, 1998.

Barmeier, Jim. *The Brain*. San Diego, CA: Lucent Books, 1996.

Brynie, Faith Hickman, *101 Questions Your Brain Has Asked About Itself but Couldn't Answer…Until Now.* Brookfield, CT: Millbrook, 1998.

Conlan, Roberta (ed.). *States of Mind: New Discoveries about How Our Brains Make Us Who We Are.* New York: Dana Press, 1999.

Funston, Sylvia and Jay Ingram. *It's All in Your Brain.* New York: Grosset and Dunlap, 1995.

Greenfield, Susan A. *The Human Brain: A Guided Tour.* New York: Basic Books, 1997.

Greenfield, Susan A. *The Human Mind Explained.* New York: Henry Holt, 1992.

Kotulak, Ronald. *Inside the Brain: Revolutionary Discoveries of How the Mind Works.* Kansas City, MO: Andrews and McMeel, 1996.

Llamas, Andreu. *The Nervous System.* Milwaukee, WI: Gareth Stevens, 1998.

Novitt-Mareno, Anne D. *How Your Brain Works.* Emeryville, CA: Ziff-Davis Press, 1995.

Paterniti, Michael. *Driving Mr. Albert: A Trip Across America with Einstein's Brain.* New York: Dial Press, 2000.

Ramachandran, V.S. and Sandra Blakeslee. *Phantoms in the Brain.* New York: William Morrow, 1998.

Rowan, Pete. *Big Head! A Book about Your Brain and Your Head.* New York: Knopf, 1998.

Van Der Meer, Ron. *The Brain Pack: An Interactive, Three-Dimensional Exploration of the Mysteries of the Mind.* Philadelphia: Running Press, 1996.

Wade, Nicholas. *The Science Times Book of the Brain.* New York: Lyons Press, 1998.

Walker, Richard. *Brain: Our Body's Nerve Center.* Danbury, CT: Grolier Education, 1998.

Web Sites

Brain Briefings
Learn more about different brain functions and diseases—
www.sfn.org/briefings/

Brain Surf
Read more about neuroscience. This site also has a link to fun facts about the brain—www.sahs.uth.tmc.edu/brainsurf/

Neuroscience for Kids
Find out more information about the brain, spinal cord, and neurons. Web site also features an experiments and activities section—
http://faculty.washington.edu/chudler/neurok.html

Probe the Brain
Map out the brain's motor cortex and read interesting facts about the brain—
www.pbs.org/wgbh/aso/tryit/brain/

Index